AUSTRALIA'S SCARIEST CREATURES

BY JOHN LESLEY

DANGEROUS SHARKS

REDBACK publishing

First published 2024 by
Redback Publishing
PO Box 357 Frenchs Forest NSW 2086
Australia

www.redbackpublishing.com
orders@redbackpublishing.com

ISBN 978-1-761400-39-1

Author: John Lesley
Editor: Caroline Thomas
Designer: Redback Publishing
Original illustrations © Redback Publishing 2024
Originated by Redback Publishing

Acknowledgements
Abbreviations: l—left, r—right, b—bottom, t—top, c—centre, m—middle
We would like to thank the following for permission to reproduce photographs (images © Shutterstock unless otherwise stated): p20-21c ; p26-27bc D Ross Robertson, Public domain, via Wikimedia Commons

NATIONAL LIBRARY OF AUSTRALIA
A catalogue record for this book is available from the National Library of Australia

CONTENTS

GREAT WHITE SHARK

Carcharodon carcharias

The great white shark had a bad reputation with people who like swimming in the ocean. The monster in the scary movie, *Jaws*, is a great white shark. Do great whites deserve this level of fear? Are they really man-eaters?

BITING

Great white sharks have killed humans. This has prompted some people to kill great whites whenever they find them in the ocean.

LIFECYCLE

Great white sharks give birth to pups that are able to swim away and look after themselves immediately. They can live for over fifty years and some grow to six metres long.

FACT FILE

Body colour: grey back and white belly
Scientific name: *Carcharodon carcharias*
Other names: White pointer; White Shark

FACT
Great white sharks can smell blood in the water kilometres away.

FACT
Great white sharks have been responsible for human deaths in Australian waters.

FOOD

Great white sharks are carnivorous. They eat fish, seals, penguins and many other types of creatures they find in the water. They will also eat dead animals they find.

HABITAT

Great white sharks live in the ocean at all depths. They can dive over a kilometre down to find food, or they can leap out of the water to catch an animal that is trying to fly or jump away from them. This is called breaching. They can live a very short while out in the air but will soon die if they do not return to sea water.

CONSERVATION

As a top predator in the ocean, the great white depends on the health of the whole ecosystem to survive. The great white is under threat at present, with numbers declining. While this sounds like good news for human swimmers, it is a serious threat to the health of the ocean.

BULL SHARK

Carcharhinus leucas

Cleaning up the pollution in Australia's rivers has led to one unwanted result. Bull sharks now swim along these rivers, where people often mistake them for great whites. Bull sharks can survive for long periods in fresh water, so if you spot a shark a long way from the ocean it is probably a bull shark.

Bull sharks have a sleek shape. They have a wide head, which is the main way to tell the difference between them and great whites.

LIFECYCLE

Bull sharks can live for over twenty years. In the summer, they swim up rivers to give birth to their pups. A young bull shark is about thirty centimetres long. When it is small, the pup is safer in a river, rather than out in the open ocean, where there are many carnivores that would like to eat it. They eventually grow to about three metres long.

FACT

Bull sharks are aggressive. They have attacked humans in rivers and harbours all around the world, including in Australia.

FACT

Bull sharks were sighted in flooded streets during the 2011 Brisbane floods.

FACT FILE

Body colour: grey back and lighter coloured belly

Scientific name: *Carcharhinus leucas*

Other names: River shark; Swan River whaler; Freshwater whaler

HABITAT

Bull sharks live in tropical and temperate oceans and rivers.

FOOD

Bull sharks are carnivores but probably do not hunt human swimmers as food. They tend to prefer smaller prey such as fish and crabs as meals. In rivers, they will eat any animal that goes into the water.

BITING

Bull sharks do bite and can cause very serious wounds.

TIGER SHARK

Galeocerdo cuvier

LIFECYCLE

The female tiger shark produces live pups. Adults grow to about five metres long and can weigh up to a tonne (1,000 kg). They can live for well over ten years.

HABITAT

Tiger sharks live in warm oceans and sometimes travel a short distance into rivers as well.

FOOD

Tiger sharks hunt and eat everything from crabs to fish, turtles, dolphins, seals and sea birds. They will also feed on dead animals in the water. Their well-developed senses allow them to hunt in the dark by sensing tiny movements in the water, as well as the electric fields created by other animals nearby. They have an acute sense of smell, particularly for blood in the water.

BITING

Tiger sharks are very dangerous and will attack a human swimmer. They will test large prey by bumping their snout against it before biting.

FACT

The tiger shark's teeth are sharp and point sideways, which gives them greater power to rip through flesh.

FACT FILE

Body colour: blue-grey with darker grey stripes
Scientific name: *Galeocerdo cuvier*
Other names: commonly called the 'man-eater' shark

The tiger shark is such a ferocious eater, that it often swallows ocean garbage.

FACT

The tiger shark is one of the three most dangerous in the world for human swimmers.

WOBBEGONG

Orectolobus

FACT

Divers who touch a wobbegong as it lies still on the sea floor are risking a sudden, nasty bite.

Wobbegongs are classified in the genus *Orectolobus*. They are sometimes called carpet sharks because of the patterns on their skin.

Wobbegongs do not roam the ocean like great whites. They prefer to wait for food to come near them and then they pounce on it. Their mottled colouring helps them to blend in with their surroundings. Sometimes they even let sand cover and hide them, then they grab any fish or crab that comes close. They have many skin flaps around their mouth, which may send them information about their surroundings. Their rounded fins are like paddles and are also useful for pushing the shark across the sea floor when hunting.

LIFECYCLE

Wobbegongs can grow to three metres long and weigh as much as a human adult. They produce live young.

HABITAT

The wobbegong, or carpet shark, lives on the sea floor in warm and temperate regions.

FACT

The name 'wobbegong' may be an Australian Aboriginal word meaning 'beard', in reference to the little flaps of skin around the shark's mouth.

FACT

Once a wobbegong bites, it will not let go, so stay clear of them if you are diving or snorkelling.

FOOD

Wobbegongs are carnivores. They eat mainly fish and crabs.

CONSERVATION

Wobbegongs used to be under threat of extinction, but their numbers have increased, and populations seem to be safe for the moment.

BITING

Wobbegongs have sharp teeth. They will bite a human if annoyed or threatened by them. Their wide, flat head covers a huge mouth, full of sharp teeth.

WHALE SHARK

Rhincodon typus

FACT

The whale shark is the biggest fish in the ocean.

The whale shark is the biggest fish in the ocean, and it can grow to over fourteen metres long. It is not a whale, but a fish with cartilage instead of hard bones in its body.

LIFECYCLE

Whale sharks can live for over eighty years. Females give birth to multiple, live pups, each up to a metre long.

FOOD

The whale shark is a filter feeder. It strains small creatures out of the water and does not hunt and kill prey the way that other sharks do. The head is very wide and heavy, as it has to house the extremely large mouth and the food-filtering structures. Whale sharks can suck in huge volumes of water, but they don't like any big animal getting into their mouth.

Since they do not have any teeth and do not hunt for food, whale sharks do not attack and bite people. However, the whale shark is so enormous, that divers swimming too close have been knocked and injured by the body or fin of a whale shark.

FACT

Whale sharks dive straight down to a depth of 2 kilometres!

FACT FILE

Body colour: dark grey with lighter coloured spots

Scientific name: *Rhincodon typus*

FACT

Human divers who get too close risk being sucked towards a whale shark's mouth by accident!

HABITAT

Whale sharks live in warm, tropical oceans.

CONSERVATION

Whale sharks are endangered. The reasons for this include:

- pollution of the oceans
- threats to their food sources from ocean warming
- increased commercial fishing that takes the same food that whale sharks eat

GREY NURSE SHARK

Carcharias taurus

Grey nurse sharks grow to about three metres long. The head is pointed, and the back is raised in a low hump.

LIFECYCLE

The female shark gives birth to live pups that can be a metre long. Adults can live for around twenty years.

HABITAT

Grey nurse sharks live in temperate seas around the coasts of Queensland, New South Wales and Western Australia. They also live in temperate oceans in other parts of the world.

FOOD

The grey nurse sharks' teeth are longer and more pointed than the triangular teeth of a great white shark. The irregular, pointed teeth stick out from the mouth, giving the shark a fearsome appearance.

FACT

Large numbers of grey nurse sharks gather to breed in 'aggregation sites'. One of these is at Wolf Rock, off Gympie in Queensland.

FACT

There are probably only a few thousand grey nurse sharks left in waters off Australia's eastern coast.

FACT FILE

Body colour: grey-brown back and light-coloured belly

Scientific name: *Carcharias taurus*

Other names: Sand tiger shark; Ragged-tooth shark

CONSERVATION

Grey nurse sharks are endangered and threatened with extinction.

BITING

Grey nurse sharks developed a reputation as man-eaters, but this was largely due to them being confused with great white sharks. They are not normally as aggressive as once thought. However, they will bite a diver or swimmer who gets in their way.

PORT JACKSON SHARK

Heterodontus portusjacksoni

Unlike the bigger sharks, the Port Jackson shark does not need to swim constantly to allow it to get enough oxygen out of the water. Its efficient gills allow it to lie still on the sea floor. Port Jackson sharks have a large, oddly shaped head, and rounded pectoral fins.

LIFECYCLE

The female Port Jackson shark lays eggs in spiral egg cases which she pushes into rock crevices. The adults grow up to two metres long.

HABITAT

Port Jackson sharks swim on long migrations around the coastal waters of Australia. They tend to stay near the sea floor, which is where they find most of their food.

FOOD

The main food sources for Port Jackson sharks are fish, crabs, sea snails and sea urchins. They have two sorts of teeth: sharp ones for biting and flat ones for crushing shells.

BITING

The Port Jackson Shark is not interested in testing a large animal with a small bite to see if it is good to eat or not. Despite this, if a person's hand, leg or arm gets too close to a Port Jackson shark's mouth, it may bite and hang on.

FACT

The two fins on the back both have a sharp spine on them, which the shark uses to defend itself.

FACT FILE

Body colour: grey-brown body with two black stripes

Scientific name: *Heterodontus portusjacksoni*

Other names: Bullhead shark

FACT

Although they are small, the Port Jackson sharks migrate many hundreds of kilometres each year.

GREAT HAMMERHEAD

Sphyrna mokarran

FACT

Hammerheads can see almost completely all around themselves.

FACT

The Hammerhead brain is the most developed of any shark. This means it is both smart and dangerous.

The defining feature of a hammerhead shark is that its eyes are at the ends of extensions that stick out from each side of the head. This adaptation improves its ability to see what is around it.

The strange, unwieldy appearance of the hammerhead shark does not make it any less fierce than its more streamlined shark relatives. The hammerhead is just as fast and dangerous.

FACT FILE

Body colour: plain grey back and lighter-coloured belly
Scientific name: *Sphyrna mokarran*

FACT

Hammerheads can sense Earth's magnetic field, and probably use this as a road map during their long migrations through the oceans.

FOOD

Hammerheads hunt for fish, crabs and squid.

LIFECYCLE

Female hammerheads give birth to numerous pups. So that the pups' eyes are not damaged, the extensions are bent backwards for protection during birth. Adults grow to about six metres long.

HABITAT

Hammerheads like to be in warm waters, both near the coast as well as in the open ocean. They often congregate in large groups of over a hundred sharks.

BITING

Hammerheads might bite humans if they find them in the water near a shoal of fish, or if there is blood in the water.

GUMMY SHARK

Mustelus antarcticus

SHARK DINNER

In a fish shop, shark is called flake. It is often deep-fried and sold as 'fish and chips' for takeaways.

Gummy sharks have been caught as food by people for thousands of years. They are still a common ingredient in human meals.

LIFECYCLE

Female gummy sharks produce eggs that hatch inside their body. The pups continue to develop there, each feeding on its own yolk sac. When they are big enough to live independently in the ocean, they are born. This is called ovoviviparous reproduction.

Gummy sharks can grow to just under two metres long, but it is the small ones that are caught by fishers for human consumption. Adult gummy sharks can live for over ten years.

HABITAT

Gummy sharks live in coastal waters all around Australia, from the tropical north to the cooler Tasmanian seas. They are often seen in very shallow water near beaches.

FACT FILE

Body colour: grey back and paler belly

Scientific name: *Mustelus antarcticus*

Other names: Smooth dog shark; Flake; Sweet William

FACT

Like all seafood, gummy shark (or flake), may contain mercury from polluted oceans.

FOOD

The gummy shark eats crabs, small fish and squid.

BITING

Gummy sharks are one of the very few sharks that are relatively safe to handle if you catch one. Fishers who find a gummy shark in their catch can end up being bitten if they put a hand too close to the shark's mouth. Although gummy shark teeth are not sharp, the bite can be painful because their jaws are very strong.

HOW ARE SHARKS SPECIAL?

ON THE MOVE

Sharks do not have lungs. They need to keep moving to get oxygen out of the water as it passes over their gills. While small sharks can stay still for a while, larger sharks, such as the great white, must move constantly or they will drown.

Sharks have cartilage instead of bone. Cartilage is a strong, flexible connective tissue that absorbs impact better than bone. Humans have cartilage in the flexible parts of their ear and nose structures

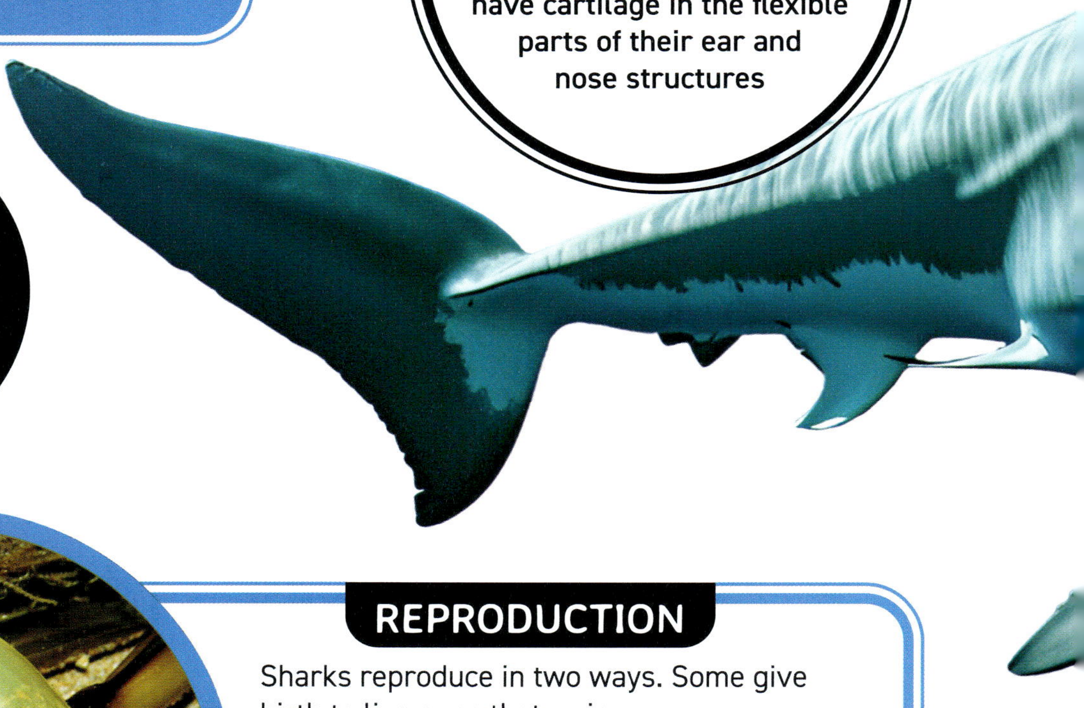

Sharks do not have scales like fish, but their skin has many tiny, sharp bumps instead

MERMAID'S PURSE

REPRODUCTION

Sharks reproduce in two ways. Some give birth to live pups that swim away as soon as they are born. Other sharks produce a leathery pouch, sometimes called a mermaid's purse, that protects the developing embryo until the baby shark hatches. These purses are sometimes found washed up on beaches.

ANCIENT

Sharks are a very ancient type of animal. They were around long before the dinosaurs, and even before there were any trees or flowers on Earth.

Sharks can feel electromagnetism from other animals around them in the ocean

Most sharks have many rows of sharp, triangular teeth. As the older, worn teeth fall out, they are replaced by a new row

Sharks are fish, not mammals like whales

SHARK FINNING

This awful practice involves cutting off sharks' fins, then dumping the shark back into the sea to die. It is illegal in Australian waters. The fins are used for soup or for traditional medicine in some parts of the world.

REMORA AND PILOT FISH

REMORA FISH

Remora fish attach themselves to sharks using a sucker to get a free ride. They eat scraps left over from the shark's meal, and keep the shark's body free of parasites.

PILOT FISH

Pilot fish often tag along with sharks. They swim out of reach of the shark's jaws but follow them to pick up leftover food and gain protection from predators. A shark that is not hungry may allow a pilot fish to swim into its mouth to eat any parasites living in there.

MORE AUSTRALIAN SHARKS

BLACKTIP SHARK
OCEANIC WHITETIP SHARK
BRONZE WHALER SHARK
BLIND SHARK
SCHOOL SHARK

SHARK ATTACKS!

Great white sharks have been responsible for the highest number of shark attacks on people, and the frequency of their attacks is getting higher.

Bull sharks and tiger sharks come in second and third in the number of sharks that have attacked people in Australian oceans and rivers.

The level of emotion involved in the reporting of shark attacks by the media makes it difficult to find out the true statistics. The best official source of data, the Australian Shark-Incident Database, is maintained by the Taronga Conservation Society Australia. Their database records shark attacks on humans dating back to 1791.

GREAT WHITE SHARK

AVOID A SHARK ATTACK

- Swim at patrolled beaches
- Swim with another person
- Don't swim when there are lots of fish in the water
- Don't swim at night, dawn or dusk
- Don't swim in water where fishers have been cleaning their catch

SHARKS: LIONS OF THE OCEAN

Large sharks are often called the lions of the ocean. This is because lions and sharks are both top predators in their environments. Being at the top of their food chains, they play important roles in keeping the animals they prey on strong and healthy.

How can that be? They eat them, but they keep them healthy? YES!

By preying on the weaker and slower animals in a species, both lions and sharks serve the purpose that is common to all top predators. They feed on the slower and weaker animals amongst their prey, which results in the fitter and faster being the ones that escape to produce more offspring. Over time, this makes the whole population of prey animals stronger.

GLOSSARY

Shark Word List

acute very precise

breaching rising up out of the water

carnivorous eating meat

cartilage structural tissue that is softer and more flexible than bone

fearsome frightening

ferocious angry and dangerous

hump bump

mottled patterned with different shapes and colours

ovoviviparous keeping eggs inside the mother's body until the young have already hatched

parasite animal that lives off another animal

pectoral around the shoulder area

predator animal that hunts another animal

prey animal that is hunted and eaten by another

pup baby shark

shoal large group of fish

sleek smooth and streamlined

temperate warm regions north and south of the Equator

tropical Equatorial regions of the world

unwieldy not well balanced

INDEX